CW01163082

Poetry For The 23rd Century

Impact Poet, Ms. JuruDaWise

Published by Ebony Enterprises 9 LLC, 2024.

POETRY FOR THE 23RD CENTURY

First edition. November 13, 2024.

ISBN: 979-8227243683

Written by Impact Poet, Ms. JuruDaWise.

Table of Contents

Dedication

I dedicate this book to the truth seekers, the deep and quiet, to lovers, and to all and any who dare to dream wide awake.

Acknowledgements

A heartfelt thank you to all the amazing people who supported and inspired this work. To all my sisters and brothers, my loved ones, friends, and community—this book wouldn't exist without your constant encouragement, feedback, and support. A special shoutout to Aubrieann, whose love and support and partnership made these poems breathe with life.

And to those who have ever doubted me, I couldn't have done it without you too.

Chapter Overviews

Overview of Chapter 1: Love & Longing

This chapter explores the raw emotions of love, longing, and passion. Whether it's the fantasy of a perfect relationship, the complications of intimacy, or overcoming doubts about love, each poem captures the powerful essence of human connection.

Delusions

Exploring fantasies of love, emotional yearnings, and the elusive feeling of finding someone perfect.

My Shining Star

A tribute to someone special, describing a newfound love that has brought light into a previously dark world.

What I Love About You

Describing the ideal lover, highlighting the feelings of affection and imagining the perfect connection.

Selfish Reasons

Contemplating the balance between love for oneself and romantic attachment, questioning priorities.

World Of Sin

The passion and intimacy shared with a lover, complicated by the presence of an ex and emotional conflict.

Love Skeptic

Overcoming doubts about love and opening oneself to new romantic possibilities.

Complicated

Confusion in relationships, navigating trust, love, and the wounds of the past.

Heart Felt

Raw emotions reflecting on loss, survival, and finding one's place in the world.

Try Harder

Perseverance through doubt, highlighting resilience in the face of challenges and relationship dynamics.

Overview of Chapter 2: Emotional Growth & Self-Reflection

Dive into the journey of self-discovery, where confusion and pain meet resilience. These poems reflect personal growth, the battle with inner demons, and the ultimate realization of self-love.

Fuzebox

Navigating confusion and internal conflict, exploring the complexity of one's own mind.

Who Are You?

A reflection on self-identity, needs versus wants, and the realization of self-love.

Problems

Struggling with inner demons and the feeling of being trapped in one's current situation, striving for something better.

Misleading

The quest for fulfillment and distractions, grappling with confusion about what brings true happiness.

IntroPerverted

A daring glimpse into unspoken desires, where passion becomes both a craving and a secret solace.

POETRY FOR THE 23RD CENTURY

Overview of Chapter 3: Society & Critique

A critical look at the world around us—these poems tackle societal norms, broken relationships, and the conflicts that arise when navigating expectations. The raw truths presented here urge readers to question and reflect on the systems we live in.

No

A reflection on limitations, questions, and doubts imposed by society, grappling with feelings of powerlessness.

Don't You See?

A critique of societal manipulation, urging people to wake up to the forces that seek to divide them.

JuruTheWise

An introspective journey that reveals wisdom through experience, unmasking truths with raw, unfiltered clarity.

Ka-Reared

A reflection on cultural roots and self-worth, where heritage anchor's identity and empowers growth.

Ex's

Calling out a former lover's behavior, reflecting on broken trust and disappointment.

Smith

Anger and heartbreak expressed through imagery of destruction, reflecting on a love that ended in chaos.

The Purge

A defiant call for freedom, shedding limitations to embrace authenticity and personal strength.

Overview of Chapter 4: Pain & Resilience

Pain is both a burden and a teacher. This chapter captures the struggle of enduring hardship while finding the strength to rise again. Through powerful imagery and unfiltered emotions, these poems portray resilience in its truest form.

Relentless Self-Reminder/NFG (No F*cks Given)

Declaring a no-fear attitude and pushing through challenges with an unwavering spirit.

Delusions

Capturing the confusion between love and longing, and the pain of unfulfilled dreams.

My Friend Pain

A poetic conversation with pain, understanding it as both an enemy and an unavoidable aspect of life.

Everyday

Emphasizing the struggle between internal darkness and resilience, striving to overcome life's obstacles.

Fate Thoughts

Unfiltered emotions that portray the struggle of staying afloat while dealing with internal battles.

Heavy Smoke

Pain becomes a mentor in resilience, transforming hardship into a foundation of inner strength.

Chapter 1:

Love & Longing

My Shining Star

I say my shining star
cause before...
inside of me was so dark
and deep in my heart, somehow
a light shone through a sliver,
a part,
I thought was obliviated from the past.
But so fast did it get repaired back anew.
I thank you my shining star,
because without you
I'm nothing more than a closed door shutting out the world.
Now the world is wide open, the possibilities are becoming endless
I picture myself in swim shorts and my future wife in a sundress
I want you – to guide my path with your light
I need you – to remind me from time to time, that you exist within me.
I love you – for always reminding me of how your love is unconditional,
even from afar.
Because you are – dust that is a part of me,
As above, so below – I can clearly now see.
My shining star.

What I Love About You

I love the way you look at me,
with your eyes, pretty and brown.
I love the way you kiss me,
Your lips being so soft and smooth.
I love the way you make me laugh and the ways you show that you care.
The way that "I love you" escapes your lips
into the thin of air.
The way you touch me.
Always sending chills down my spine.
I love when you spend your time with me
I hope that forever you'll be mine.
When I find you one day,
or in some years.
What I don't love about you,
is that you're not real.
There can't possibly be
a person out there for me
who also wants to grow and evolve
into a healthy human being.
But maybe I can still dream.
Cause what I love about you the most,
is that you may not exist in real life, but
through my mind's eye, I can always visit you when I sleep.

Selfish Reasons

I can be selfish
Fuck all the rest
I look out for me
Like the scope for all the feds
I neglect the world
To listen to tunes
I know I told a few I'd call.
That was thirty minutes ago.
I'm staring at my phone
Staring back into a pic of us two.
Like what should I do?
I told myself never again!
But here I am having all these feelings,
for a person like you.
Asking myself all these questions
Like is it false or is it true?
For selfish reasons,
Is it wrong to choose my happiness over you?

World Of Sin

I love your accent
How you stick out posted on the wall,
tryna look tough as nails with big metal balls
My new accent, accentuated.
And when we get situated
You know you can always get it baby.
Call me at work just to let me know
when I get home,
you gon' ride it, dicks overrated
Tonight, it's just me and you
In our own skin we gon
lay up
fuck up,
stay up,
post up
NFG to our haters in this world of sin.
Slowly trace my lips
Down the side of your neck
When your away your all I think about,
You make me wet
How can I forget?
I slipped up once
and I don't want to do anything else that I'd regret.
Cause right now, I'm sitting here with my ex
tryna be friends, but she just wants the sex

this probably won't end well
I don't know what I'm doing.
Theres no rules to the game of life.
No steps.
I think I lost the map to life on my crash-landing in.
Laden in my bin.
In this crazy world of sin.

Love Skeptic

There's no rules to the game of life;
No Steps.
All I know is that you are what's currently next
Is this a pre-screening to the rest of my life,
how my thoughts are before a paper
Like a pre-text?
You over qualify for the job, and I'm not easy to get into...
...but... you've answered all my questions
like a pre-test.
Is this love true?
Let's see if you can beat the love skeptic.

Complicated

I hate it all
Waiting for the system to fall
Waiting for the crumbling of my wall
Almost feeling like a Lost soul.
Presently present,
in the presence
of the present,
with no present.
Raise your hand if you're complicated.
Great. Another heaven-sent.
I got to stop trying to be something I'm not
Finally, someone attempts to see me and not just what I got.
I'm afraid I will hurt her
I'm afraid that she'll make her mark
But all that consideration is out the window.
She made her mark and tore what I had left of my fuckin heart!
I swear after you, I'll duct tape myself up
Don't come back looking for love,
bitch beware, you got me fucked up!
Let's be clear
I can't stand my ex now,
So, no X-Games this year
Looking out for me
Cause I'm out there somewhere
Even though I am right here.

Will you love me or what I do for you?
That's what I fear.
I look past my own past
Perpetually
Looking for my soul that was once truly unconditionally loving
But I'm at some random ass party
Doing drugs, while smiling
They don't tell you it all plays a bigger role,
Cause if you speak up, undercover addicts start trolling
And will literally consider you a mole.
Dependent on Independence Day.
Haha!
Fuck it!
I'll roll me a J-Back anyways.
Come to the crib, its 420 here everyday
We can smoke the stress away.
Turn yourself in straight, in here
Leave us turning out gay & quite queer.
Yep, the complicated way.

This

There's something different in the air.
The naked eye enshrouded is blind
But there's still something there.
This...
...is new to me.
Old duck, yep, it's clear.
But still, there's something tangible here.
This... feeling...
When I'm around you,
it's a complete scare.
Numbers sometimes align
Time turns to my side
The sky shines sunny bright
and somehow everything goes just right.
It's hard to believe that this is happening in real life,
and not in some fairytale
But it's here.
This... longing...
Lingering, hanging thick in the air
So much unspoken feelings, it's too hard to scale
Are you someone sent from above,
to finally show me what it's like to love and be loved?
This ...isn't always clear.

Heart Felt

Yeah, I miss you all the time even though it's hard to admit it.
You almost had me there, glad my heart wasn't fully in it.
I thank the universe almost every day that I'm still here, fucking living.
Even though it still feels like I'm just dying on the surface.
No one really fucking gets it.
No one really pays a fucking attention.
Never shot a metal weapon, just verbal and still...
No one really fucking listens.
At least I'm out here trying,
while you're still over there, fucking bitchin'.
I'm just tryna make an honest living,
for my mom and fucking siblings.
I'm 22 and young and things my G, are finally clicking.
This weed got me way too lifted
and money has me addicted.
Watching out 'cause some of these girls are fucking twisted.
Have you all in your emotions and going through the motions.
Shit makes you wanna call your own biological sex,
Triflin, hoe ass, bitches!
But my tongues trigga finger is itchin.
Cause while I shoot for the stars,
you shoot to sabotage.
I can hear your metal clickin.
Though the bullet will never reach me out here on fucking Marz,
dancing with the cosmic stars

Finally, having heartfelt conversations.

Try Harder

All these thirsty ass bitches
want to be treated like they're classy.
But if I spend my money on you, it might make me trashy by association,
and I'm not tryna be sassy.
Babygirl said what's sexy about me
Is my intelligence.
So, I showered her with compliments
when I saw her words every Wknd.
She Earned It.
Old dudes hate.
New dudes tryna flex.
Bitches talk shit.
the devil is always watching,
She's mad that she's my ex.
She's wishing she played her games right
Ho must've forgot I'm the Queen at chess
You're gonna have to try harder
to break me, hurt me, or spite me,
in order to beat the best.

Chapter 2:

Emotional Growth & Self-Reflection

Fuzebox

Sometimes I'm confused.
My brain becomes a Fuzebox.
With no key, no map, no answer to unlock.
Go with your gut on this one.
Follow your heart.
Doesn't matter if you get hurt,
at least it's a start.
That's what I tell myself
You know, to reassure?
But sometimes that doesn't work.
Fuzebox, under pressure.
Intruders invade it.
You know, questions and speculations?
And sometimes my Fuzebox can't think straight,
No circulation.
So, to get intruders out
I HAVE to overthink.

I stay really quiet and calm on the outside
You know, to concentrate?
But that doesn't work
It just makes all things that can go bad, worse.
I'll roll a blunt, or read a book.
You know, to levitate?
I'll learn how to protect myself.

I don't wanna get hurt.
By jerks who find it cool to sell false hugs
and follow dumb 106 Park bums,
that wanna wear fake lashes all day and twerk.
Not me, I just mind my business and work,
You know like the government says, to compensate?
Tuh. A Fuzebox quirk.

Who are you?

I see her in the distance.
A faint whisper in my ear
A blurry picture I can't always see,
but in my heart holding dear.

I always get what I want, but
I'm always feeling that I'm missing what I need.
Walking my heart around blindly.
Showing it mainly what my eyes see.

Confusing my wants and thinking they're my needs
Focusing on nothing I know is truly important
And it's making my heart bleed.

Life has a funny way of teaching you
That what you think you know,
may not even be true.

That what you thought you liked,
could be the very thing you hate too.
That what you want,
isn't necessarily what you need.
And that maybe my quest for the perfect one is pointless,
Because, there will never be a perfect tree.

Love is the key to life.
Knowing thyself will bring my soul closer to me.

Problems

Sometimes I realize,
How small I really am
In this big ass world we live in.

How do I fit in?
War amongst my own
When the real war should be fighting for
our minds, bodies, and souls!
Too many strings on us,
like puppets, we're controlled.
Own yourself
and you can have the greener side to life too.
Nothing but everything in this world is taboo.
What's for me isn't for you.
But believe in yourself dude.
Minds like gods.
Float past the bullshit
and I'll admit!
Women take me on power trips.

While my zips give me power lifts.
I'm unguarded, outspoken, and slanderish
with power lips.
I got my girl sucking slowly on my swollen clit
Shorty thinks she really knows me.

Does what I really want.
I guess it's safe to say, she can really be "my bitch".
Though she looks like
she might be the one to forfeit the title wifey,
with her immature bullshit.
I really need to get my shit together.
22 at home with moms
is like winning best photo,
only for it to be photobombed.
Every time I take 10 steps forward,
I feel like I go back nine.
This stupid house traps me.
Slowly it tries to transform me
to become this unholy being
riddled with holes, trying to become whole.
While I slowly feel myself unraveling,
with this place driving me pinche Loca!
I don't know if I'm meant to be
in a stooped dazed mentality,
straddling depression,
constantly, defending the saner part of me?
Or am I doomed to fatally face against the darker side of me?
I'll cry myself to sleep silently,
while I overthink.
But only for a week, before I realize
I need to get a grip and get from in front of me.
But these thoughts are tormenting me
Haunting my pockets daily.
"WHATS OUT THERE FOR ME!?", I scream.
Echoes of my voice cascades and then careens .

I'm all by myself.

I wasn't ready to be left standing alone in the moonbeam.
Not for this, no not at all.
What makes me so great?
Stop asking me that question, that I currently don't know!
I guess whatever is different from y'all?
Or whatever I can pull out my head and show?
It doesn't always encourage me to stand tall.
Anger management is needed (I know)
or maybe I should sell drugs and play ball.
Success and wealth.
Long lasting health.
Love your roots forever.
Trust only guts.
Bust her down and cuddle?
Nah. She only wants my bucks
Fuck it. I'll go start my own shit
No more giving out free fucks.
Long live my legacy
My mind lands, in a world full of mines,
all to expose my problems?
Well like the property I hope to gain,
I'm learning to own it and solve them.

Misleading

I don't know where I'm really going.
Show me where the girls are with their ass and titties showing.
The golden girls who fuck with dudes with big banks,
without the flashy throwing.
Top shelf growing
Obie doobie rolling
Skurt-skurt crash the imaginary Rari
I hope you have 5-star towing
I'm feeling like having a party
We fingerpainting, touching and glowing.
Show me the girls who suck slowly on your fingers
Where you already know where it's going
Where she doesn't mind if I beat it up
she likes it mean
Eat it up
Clean it up.
Roll it up.
Bounce out.
Then spark it up.
The girls who shine bright like a high beam
Proud savages making that Guap
She seems to be on the winning team.
lets shoot our shot
Swallow fear and step up chump.
Excuse me Miss,

Can I Lead?

IntroPerverted

Daydreaming constantly about the possibilities of you and me
I want to see you spread your legs
Slip inside your hot oven
turn me into your baked goods
Finger fucking
Clit sucking
Cream on my fingers
Watching you suck it off
Tease me until I get off
Deep throat my fingers
One by one
Back chills
Pussy pulse
We at your moms crib for dinner
So fuck me for the thrills
100% raining energy at last
Guess that makes you 100% real
Synchronized souls
Something to feel
Forget about my past
With your lust I can heal
But these perverted thoughts may just be my only meal.
Food for my thoughts I never tell you, when you ask me how I feel.

Chapter 3:

Societal Critique's

No

Feelings
Un-describable
Un-writable
Un-comprehensible
Deep down inside
Unheard of
Unspoken
Places I wanna be
Never will be able to
Won't happen
Can't possibly happen
Questions.
Unanswered
Ignored
They're all dumb anyways
No.
Don't speak
Don't listen
Don't hear
Don't worry
Don't fear
Yes.
Hurt
Pain and agony

Don't You See?

You make us feel inferior
Because you know that we are intellectually superior
You know you can't break us on the outside
So you've moved to the interior.
My people don't you see?
Rise up and make that mental barrier.
It's critical
No data, but I'm sending this message
Cause I'm the carrier
Don't you see?
Armed with knowledge
No drugs
No weapons for protection
It's what make us
That much scarier.
They've turned us against ourselves.
Don't you see?
We are our own terror.
I'll pass the light to your darkness.
Don't you see?
Here, let's make it clearer.

JuruTheWise

Yea I know I'm a beast.
I'm hungry watch me eat this feast
Tryna get some V
But don't eat it
if it's got yeast
Eek
I'm Meek
Tryna make a mill by next week
But It's bleak
I don't turn cheeks
I just spread 'em and shit on beats
Creep in between them sheets
Then chop you up cleverly
like some meat
Pause.
I can't control my intake of the trees
Stomping out the grass snakes,
leaving all the tall weeds.
Let's blaze up the fire
there's no need for greed
Real Representer of peace
Like my girl says to me
Sheesh
Please don't make this harder
I'm here for your health like water

It's vital
A wave of haze
Should be plaqued and my title.
Peace is the mission
Yes, Major Paper
Is always what's final
Moon rocks in my papers cradled
Saucing getting chicken you may need a ladle
Soup mama bringing you happiness
Through a smile
I saw your face
looks like it's been a while
I'm here to nurture you my child
Only the realest truths
For the brave and wild
Changing the world eye views
From those black and white tiles
To what's real and worthwhile
The world is almost as real as those X-Files
Ima X out the men in this world that's vile
Makes you wanna throw up life
It's that bile
Beware Evil men and women
I'ma be the one to Bring yo ass to trial
That Golden G.U.E Child
To me, a Goddess Unleashing her Ether is mild
Hitting harder than an asteroid
Droppin nuggets of knowledge on roadblocks
for miles and miles
Camera snaps me faking a smile
I'll never pretend to like you
if I do that's sly

Why lie?
Why be that guy?
Why do I see people constantly inserting drama into their lives?
Hear my cry
I'm a bit shy
But my thoughts speak volumes
I came from the sky
And I'm searching for my heirlooms
Instead, I found weed so dope feels like I took a hit of shrooms
Never am hive mindedly blind and I'm always on the know ledge grind
An A-Bomb filmed and not destroyed within itself?
Boom.
Guess how my brotha's and sista's be acting like these days?
Coons.
It's a problem, I took upon myself to start solving
Cause who else will?
We'll just keep getting footed the bill
Residential homies aren't aware of the impending doom
"Presidential" fools sitting in their fat ass wallets cars and house
there's no way he's making moves on me,
to invest in our people and improve.
But be so quick to hang out with sketchy, backstabbing, white dudes?
What are you scared of?
What "the man" is gonna do?
Shit, I get it, sometimes me too,
But fuck that!
I'm not gonna go out playing a whack ass game like Boo-Boo Da Fool
Use ya tools!
Don't be generic & artificial like these boxed up schools
They tricked us and tripped us it's true
But never let the thunder shake ya lightening loose
The thunder is your blunder

Throw that shit like Zeus
Striking the hearts of millions on the path to truth
Unbiased untouched original proofs
I'm going hard like concrete
I'm too wise to refute

Ka-Reared

They said I'm not gang related
so, I don't know about the struggle
Somehow not killing my brotha
equates to me not knowing how to hustle
She wants me to put in that work
And to pay attention to her
She gets on my nerves
her back and forth mood swerves
that's so subtle
It makes me clinch and pull a face muscle
so I sit at my desk and do Chinese puzzles
to un-fuddle
the muddle
With my thoughts I wrestle,
Play back my playlist
then reshuffle,
sip on Bacardi as I enjoy my kush shuttle
I broke out of my cage and my lips are unmuzzled
It's been so long since I cared, as a woman I grew stubble
I don't guzzle to forget
I crack knuckles and start scuttles
Up in my castle if I see you throwing rubble
With a sniper I'll muffle your ruffles
Hit my man Jug up cause he like to juggle them shovels
Theres nothing you can say to convince me

IMPACT POET, MS. JURUDAWISE

I'm the master of rebuttals
But my name doesn't spell out trouble
that's why I'm always packed with duffle's
I'll leave this place and live in Brussels,
Sippin fine liquor in the tub with bubbles
Meet and greet morning huddles
At night with my wife kissin with cuddles
My money long and comes to me in abundant bundles
I chuckle while the words you choose show how much you fumble and tumble
Shooting dudes up instead of being humble
Flexing how small your brain is instead of them real muscles
I see how humans really operate
I can see from Jupiter with a Hubble
My words bury deep like underground tunnels,
that funnel energy that's sensible.
I'm sensei $tona whose inside her eternal jungle
I captured the capsule of the cradled devil
The paddle to label the former a trickster
Not an oracle
But you take his word as official
Now ladies raise the D up to a pinnacle
This shit is horrible
Now it's becoming earth global
If you believe in that sort of thing,
Your liable to be dazzled
by these fake "essentials" that's fatal
The winds that all blow in my direction
are cardinal
my vision becomes blurred
Between my two and one eye I toggle
Its substantial the initial jangle from the comparable symbol

That's agile like a burning candle
My drip hot that's why your girl screaming my name like a kettle
I sizzle you settle
I'm a spectacle that's liable to pop
Like I'm your Kernal
I'm your rival like a marshal whose moral compass is corrupted and unstable
You can hear it through the cackle I ensemble
I'm that able
In my eyes you see the twinkle
The sparkle never dwindles
I know it's all possible
You gotta hack life though cause it's a riddle
Use your tools to make it vocal
Try to dabble in things you don't know
Don't live life baffled or shackled
Taking in the new-new at a trickle
All the visuals are vital
Theres no time to quarrel
Turn your channels on and see me with the liberals
Though, their rivals, I know they are all just mortals
that tremble tryna counsel the social vessel
My message is done.
Excuse me as I jump back through my portal

Ex's

You're still selfish
Trying to grab my heart again
I'm looking at you struggling and helpless
Faced made up and I'm disgusted
My gut was right
I don't know why I never trusted it.
I see right through your hidden lines;
Your hidden lies.
Girl your X-ed out.
No more games to be played.
Bitch your Busted.

Smith

Got my anger out
obliviated
Terminated
No one guards the gates to my heart
From the start there were one million and one
but for you
there was none.
My heart took a chance
but was broken before the first dance.
Now my heart is rapping
Like I ever had a Chance.
Feelings blasted by back handed actions into a million pieces,
No more Mr. and Mrs. Smith now, call me Mr. Smithers
shiver in ye knickers
For you will pay for calling me some "uppity know-it-all nigger"
Feelings like cars careened after we've caused a scene that's turned obscenely mean,
Now my hopes of us on a float are remote and have flown out the window,
into smothered covered embers, wind gusted into smithereens.

The Purge

I'm tryna purge myself from Facebook
I'm tryna find out how your face looks
Connect to people in the real world
instead of my new Nook
What's going on in the world?
Is everything I was ever taught even real?
Young gods going to demon school hate it
I know exactly how they feel
Bright ones left to shine in the dark
Most never shining enough to be revealed
Man, like what is the deal?
It's too surreal
Why are people (still)
fighting for meals?
Why does it all have to be concealed,
like the weapons we carry,
that's licensed to kill?
Occupying hearts in this mind-filled
world with mindless folk,
who rig minefields.
Some whistle blow from Germany
to Seinfeld.
Dystopian, elopian, annoying Americans.
Who go around and flaunt like clowns
and show themselves being embarrassing.

Like "look at me I got it all I'm a Caucasian.
I represent my country that fucked over natives and the land for generations."
A country where you can pretend to be crazy and get paid for it.
The mentally unstable never get a caused fought for that's legitimate.
Cause the psycho sociopaths keep causing it.
The current state of the world, makes me (literally) sick
I'm surprised I made it without vomit
While I was flying faster to save this destination, like a comet
Wish I could commit to the teachings taught in Kemet.
No room for negative comments about it.
I'll use what I got as I pick up what's left,
and show you how I can flaunt it.
My task on this earth is quite daunting
C'mon lets grab the choppers and get on it
A tank to blow away the banks
Yeah,
now I'm really blowin hunnids
Now take a second look,
it's gonna be destructive
I'm coming in politically incorrect and disruptive
Theres no discussion
Cause you muthafuckas
Are always tryna keep me tucked in
Always using my people as a last resort for these under delivered promises,
I know your bluffing.

I see that there's this distorted type of loving,
that is evilly manifesting, like an infection
that needs healing and deep self-love correcting...

Before it's too late and we Transition into something not human.

Chapter 4:

Pain

&

Resilience

Relentless Self-Reminder/NFG (No Fucks Given)

Stay relentless
C'mon Jae, don't you doubt yourself,
cause your doubting greatness.

I realize I should've realized this a long time ago...
But I'm always fashionably late,
please excuse my lateness.
Now that I'm shining again,
I've realized we live in darkness.
I've accepted the fact that I'm different.
Going left, while the rest go right.
In a sea of fishes, I try to dethrone my ego
and swallow my shallow pride.
to release my weaknesses and fear
instead of being a cowardice and hiding.
I planned a surprise for this shorty
Only to find out I'm disliked by the family.
My own estranged uncle,
butting his head into my business and causing unnecessary friction
Cause he sees we happy
I really couldn't believe it.
But...
His bullshit wasn't a surprise to me.
When you got something to hide,

you rush to expose others attentively,
in hopes that it'll make your dusty dirt a better disguise,
to somehow lessen the stink.
Let's keep it real though.
See, fake souls I reveal from a dot of ink, to minimize
an agitated King Croc, enough to snap back and head snatch
to make you eat your own shitty lies, to your own fateful demise.
Play dumb games, win stupid prizes.
Stay blind if you want.
My open eyes
see between the conservative lines,
decoding the hidden spies,
of unsolicited rumors, that you tried.
NFG to my dysfunctionally, disfigured family members, who partake in the divisive shenanigans.
I'm cutting off all the ties!

Delusions

Delusions –
Me and you together
Not for worse, but for better
Conclusions –
Wait for your heart
To be mine, for a start
Intrusions –
Speculations of "why" imitations
But intimidation leads to persuasion?
Explosions –
Of feelings; explodes into a cloud
And blindness normal; eyes enshroud.
Conversations –
What if you were to leave him?
Why can't you delete him?
Questions –
why, when, how?
cause, never, NOW!
Delusions –
of me and you together
Carving our name in a tree;
You and me 4ever.

My Friend Pain

Pain, suffered through
Endless pain, suffered through
Ignored the bliss of organized pain
Deflected what reflected
Ol' Plain Jane pain
But I wouldn't let it,
I drove pain insane.
And because of what I wouldn't let it gain
pain swore revenge on me,
yes, pain did.
Probably, even on my future kids
Cause of what I did and didn't let pain do
I suffered through,
what pain can do.
No.
What it did to me.
No.
I categorize those separately.
I was so afraid to let pain in
and pain was mad at me
because pain was really my friend.
Instead, I befriended an emotion
who was neither a cute little puppy,
or beautiful white dove.

I turned to the sworn enemy instead,
and pain was trying to warn me of love.

Everyday

Every day is a struggle
I hide in plain sight like a wizard among muggles
I wish I could just pack duffle's on the double
No work life or drama, or girl to juggle.
Be out in a luxury sedan burning rubber.
Instead, I'm stuck with a family that doesn't love each other
and 23 still stuck babysitting my sisters and brothers.
Even when in the bathroom is my mother
I have a lot of pain and knowledge that seems to smother
Me, while I try to sleep,
but follows me into the nether realms of conscious bells,
where you see, and forget the magic spells
that's keeping you grid locked to wake up,
never to tell,
what was exposed to you in hell.
You muthafuckas.
Back to heaven I awaken just to find out my reality is a Cell.
It makes up all that is life for eternity and yells
how humanity, drains its wishing well
The worst clientele.
A to-do list keeps me from my shell,
and I wish I'm better able to tell
my thoughts more, than just sit in my mind
content to dwell.
I want to love myself so I can love you too...

...but it seems like my love is all you ever wanna do.
That makes me mad at you.
Or feel like I'm a foolish tool.
A divine mind seeing what's less than cool
whipped topping,
it's always finger-swiped first,
then they find the real Sheol.
Bite down and you realize life tastes better with an understanding of the two.
I'm silent and clazzy,
listening to jazzy tunes.
In my favorite timberland boots,
smooth leather moves.
You have to buy em,
but I place the clues
for you to find,
like Steve and Blue.
Salt and Pepper sue's
when it's not on the plate of colors.
But do you really want to be on the silver spoon?
Everyone seems to want to be devoured soon.
A rush to eternal tombs.
Souls feeling lost in gloom,
a sinful doom.
In my mind, I made more room
for the understanding of those
who elude us and fool us using brooms.
Sweeping aside all the old news
To push fear mongering fools
in music, movies, and broadcasted radio waves,
advertising in schools.
Creating mindfully mindless robotic

soul-less zombies, like BOO!
What's in YOUR box of tools?
I don't got much but some Tech N9nes and Jay Electronica's.
I get nervous when you ask me questions and shuffle my shoes.
I'll end up alive now
More surprised? How?
The earth is always enshrouded in clouds
Is it wrong that I uplift my crown?
Let's ponder this!
No need to ask some expert scientists
They always lie to us...
Wait! Aren't we born intelligent?
Why can't we solve our own problems,
and not seek out external enlightenment?
This is what I'd contemplate if I had a Cabinet
full of bright men and women who understand
under the surface realities,
As they would have known back then...
is this insight too much for most of this dimension's hue-mans?
I'm slashing all my foes heads off with just a simple pen!
A big ass mouth spitting flames of shame,
they may take a while to understand.
Though to my depths, there is no end.
Sometimes I feel like I'm my only best friend.
I'm in this world to become one.
I mean soulfully win.
Until you overstand
I suggest you sit down humble one and learn what I'm saying.
I try not to mumble.
Even when I know my stomach grumbles,
forcing me to start rumbles with the universe.
A one song that moves around in one verse.

I look up in time to see I need to swerve.
Back on course,
I'm in my fates face like an old perv.
Pop me on your tv instead of those Perc's
I know reality sometimes hurts.
I've gone berserk, but
I promise I'm not a jerk.
These are just those gifted and lifted
$tona perks
My healings for your hurts.

Fate Thoughts

She's lost, independent
With no dependents
She's as delicate as a rose petal, with no nutrients.
No substance
No distance
No more second chances
No last dances.
Teeth a bit crooked,
her soul may need some braces.
Brace yourself for
the heart pounding races
Addicted to love like a drug
Women with a little bit of make-up, that don't look like clown faces.
If you have a headache, your temple
Is my fingers favorite placement
After me girl there's no replacement
With the love I got and the love your taking
Yet I don't think this was love,
But lustful and wishful thinking
From both of us not even thinking
That being with a girl that looks like a boy
Is something you find fun, taboo, and even kinky
But I'm not a freak show, layaway display
Or maybe I'm just overthinking
I mean I'm just saying.

I thought our fates may have been aligned but
instead, I was left with lessons of self-reflections.

Heavy Smoke

Smoke heavy
chest don't fail me.
I pray daily
especially when I need some money.
El loco I'm crazy,
and sometimes lazy.
only cause I never worry
bout my paper or my lady
things getting kinda hazy
time to face me
Can't erase me
grinding brazy
my squad sprazy
when you disrespect me
Classy cammy
yakuza clanny
We come out nightly
Light your spliff up brightly
Always with a quarter of tree
Everything you regard of me
Highly
Never smiley
Yet I'm always funny
When it comes to knocking your brains out like a dummy
I need some Pepto,

I'm in her tummy
'Cept she never running to bathrooms
Cause I'm not runny
Kinda cuddly
Big D like
Dud Dudley
Baby hold me
I got big things in the morning
7 cycles 24 snoring
Big banking and bank going
I'm really getting all this bank rolling
while still ten toeing.
No ratchet hoeing
I'm truly Golden
Always Outspoken
Driven to make the world wholly
Connected
To the divine mostly
Never boasting
In the dark I'm always learning
Love yearning
Soul burning
Stomach churning
When I look all around me
I hate the ugly,
but that doesn't mean
another's eye doesn't see you beautifully.
Why can't we embrace all that comes
Naturally?
Fundamentally
There's always something to discuss morally
Orally

I convey these Goddess thoughts
On these paper leaves, especially off Her golden tree.
Powerlifts She gives me daily.
I feel so amazing thankfully.
I'm raising up these frequencies.
I'm low-key up,
like Loki.
Gas in my lungs, is why I'm always floating.
I'm flamboyant and quite annoying, if you haven't noticed.
I don't know it all, yet I feel all knowing.
Maybe because I know where I'm going
and on my way
my words paint a picture of what I'm showing.
My mom's kids glowing
Your undeserved hate we're towing
No suing.
We know you just need some deep internal healing.
Here my friend, have some of this tea I've been brewing.
Cause you're my homie
and my people are growing in this movement.
A Spoken Space was born,
A Safe Space To Be Heard,
for I know this world feels torn.
We can still stay connected
through the disconnection,
if we chose to love one another more.
I know our hearts are sore
but we GOTTA care about each other before
we start another war.
Then we ALL will get packed together under the floorboards
Sending our soldiers overseas, just for them to be kicked overboard.
Sure, we could choose each other to ignore

but it should be Love Galore.
So I'm giving out my love these days, more & more.
Smoke heavy
Chest don’t fail me
I pray daily
especially when I need some healing.
El loca, am I crazy?
cause will I ever get back that same loving?
Mann, that part is always a maybe
I guess I’ll remain patient, while I continue to do the Great Work,
and Smoke heavy.

Don't miss out!

Visit the website below and you can sign up to receive emails whenever Impact Poet, Ms. JuruDaWise publishes a new book. There's no charge and no obligation.

https://books2read.com/r/B-A-PAQQC-TKYDF

BOOKS 2 READ

Connecting independent readers to independent writers.

About the Author

Ms. JuruDaWise—also known as **Janiece Spence**—is an Impact Poet with roots in **Upstate New York**. She combines urban storytelling with lyrical depth, creating poetic works that bridge emotion, imagination, and societal reflection. Now based in **Eastern Washington**, she is the founder of **A Spoken Space**, a creative outlet that fosters safe, expressive environments for artists and communities. Her work reflects both **personal growth and public critique**, offering a raw yet sophisticated voice in modern poetry.

Read more at www.aspokenspace.com.

About the Publisher

As a self-publisher under Ebony Enterprises 9 LLC, my purpose is to amplify diverse voices and foster profound connections through written word. Each book I publish reflects my commitment to personal creativity, personal growth, and social impact, providing readers with raw, sophisticated and authentic expressions. I aim to build bridges across communities, inspiring change and sparking dialogue that resonates across generations.

Milton Keynes UK
Ingram Content Group UK Ltd.
UKHW041939241124
451423UK00001BA/213

9 798227 243683